The New Neighbors

Mary Ann Thomas

NEIGHBORHOOD READERS

Rosen Classroom Books & Materials™

New York

I have a new neighbor.

He doesn't look like me.

He doesn't live in the same kind of house.

He doesn't wear the same kind of clothes.

He doesn't eat the same kind
of food.

But he is my friend.
We play ball.

We ride bikes.
He really is like me!